Aberdeenshire Library and Information Service
www.aberdeenshire.gov.uk/libraries
Renewals Hotline 01224 661511

15 MAY 2010

18 OCT 2019

1 2 NOV 2019

GREEN, Jen

Rivers

weblinks

You don't need a computer to use this book. But, for readers who do have access to the Internet, the book provides links to recommended websites which offer additional information and resources on the subject.

You will find weblinks boxes like this on some pages of the book.

weblinks

For more information about a specific topic, go to www.waylinks.co.uk/series/GeogDetective/Rivers

waylinks.co.uk

To help you find the recommended websites easily and quickly, weblinks are provided on our own website, **waylinks.co.uk**. These take you straight to the relevant websites and save you typing in the Internet address yourself.

Internet safety

↗ Never give out personal details, which include: your name, address, school, telephone number, email address, password and mobile number.

↗ Do not respond to messages which make you feel uncomfortable – tell an adult.

↗ Do not arrange to meet in person someone you have met on the Internet.

↗ Never send your picture or anything else to an online friend without a parent's or teacher's permission.

↗ If you see anything that worries you, tell an adult.

A note to adults
Internet use by children should be supervised. We recommend that you install filtering software which blocks unsuitable material.

Website content

The weblinks for this book are checked and updated regularly. However, because of the nature of the Internet, the content of a website may change at any time, or a website may close down without notice. While the Publishers regret any inconvenience this may cause readers, they cannot be responsible for the content of any website other than their own.

WAYLAND

Rivers

Jen Green

WAYLAND

The Geography Detective Investigates series:
Your Local Area

For more information on this series and other Wayland titles,
go to www.madaboutbooks.co.uk

First published in Great Britain in 2006 by Wayland, an
imprint of Hachette Children's Books

Editor: Hayley Leach
Designer: Simon Borrough
Maps and artwork: Peter Bull
Cartoon artwork: Richard Hook
Consultant: John Lace

British Library Cataloguing in Publication Data

Green, Jen
    Rivers. - (The geography detective investigates)
    1.Rivers - Juvenile literature
    I. Title
    551.4'83

ISBN-10: 0750248165
ISBN-13: 978-0-7502-4816-7

Picture acknowledgements
The publishers would like to thank the following for permission to
reproduce their pictures:
Aerofilms.com 11; Corbis (Ariel Skelley) 4 (Arthur Morris) 14
(Bryn Colton/Assignments Photographers) 28 (Charles & Josette
Lenars) 25 (China Photos/Reuters) 19 (Dave G. Houser) 9, 23
(Galen Rowell) 8, 15 (Gavriel Jecan) 5 (John Farmar/Cordaiy Photo
Library Ltd) 12 (Jon Sparks) 13 (Julie Meech/Ecoscene) 17 (Lester
Lefkowitz) 18 (London Aerial Photo Library) 22, 27 (Marc
Garanger) 13 (Michael Freeman) 21 (Michael St. Maur Sheil) 25
(Niall Benvie) cover and 10 (Nick Hawkes; Ecoscene) 24 (Patrick
Ward) 20 (Peter Turnley) 16, 18 (Reuters) 5, 26 (Scott T. Smith) 29;
Mary Evans Picture Library 22.

Contents

Words that appear in **bold** can be found in the glossary on page 30.

SAFETY FIRST
Make sure you ask an adult to help you when you are working near water. Always take care when you are close to the water's edge.

What are rivers?

Rivers are channels of fresh water flowing downhill, pulled by gravity. Rivers give life to the land they flow through, providing vital water for plants, animals, fish and people.

People use rivers to have all sorts of fun, including fishing, canoeing and white-water rafting.

The geography detective, Sherlock Bones, will help you to delve into the mysteries of rivers. Whenever you see Sherlock Bones, you'll find a mystery to solve. Answers are given on page 31.

Rivers are found all over the world. Most rivers begin in hills or mountains and end in the sea or a lake. They start off as small streams and gradually get bigger. In countries with plenty of rain, such as Britain, rivers flow throughout the year. In hot countries, such as Africa and the Middle East, some rivers dry up at certain times of year when there is not much rain.

Rivers provide habitats for plants and all sorts of creatures, including fish, birds, mammals, frogs, crabs and crocodiles. Rivers are also vital to humans, providing us with water for drinking and washing, and for farms and industry. We use rivers to generate electricity, and to transport goods and people from place to place.

Some rivers are considered holy. People bathe in the River Ganges in India to cleanse both their body and their soul.

Rivers are a precious resource, but people don't always look after them properly. For centuries, rivers have been used as a dumping ground for waste. Unfortunately, waste dumped upstream harms plants, animals and people downstream. It is vital that we take care of rivers, both for our own sake and for river life.

DETECTIVE WORK

Study a local map to find out about the rivers in your area. Find out how long the nearest river is, and where you are on its course.

Rivers have many uses, including for transport. Docks and factories line many rivers as they reach the sea.

FOCUS ON

The world's greatest rivers

The River Nile is the world's longest river, flowing through North Africa for 6,671 km. However, the River Amazon in South America contains the greatest amount of water of any river. Europe's longest river is the Volga, at 3,531 km long.

Why do you think some rivers dry up altogether?

CAMMELL LAIRD
SHIPBUILDERS ENGINEERS & REPAIRERS

How do rivers begin?

The place where a river starts is called the **source**. Rivers begin as streams high in hills or mountains fed by springs, lakes or **glaciers**. As the river flows downhill it is joined by more streams or minor rivers, called **tributaries**, which add to its waters. The point where two rivers join is called a **confluence**. The widest point is often near the **mouth** or **outlet**, where the river empties into the sea or a lake.

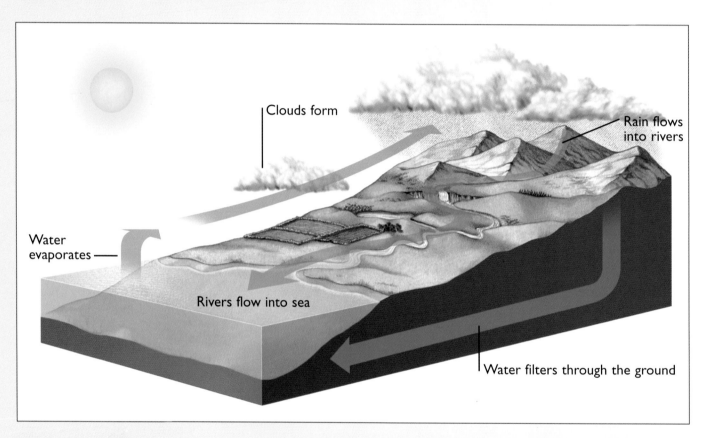

Clouds form

Rain flows into rivers

Water evaporates

Rivers flow into sea

Water filters through the ground

Water moves between the air, sea and land in an endless circle called the water cycle.

A river and all its streams and tributaries make up a **river system**. The whole area drained by the river and its tributaries is called the **drainage basin**.

Rivers are part of a natural cycle in which water moves between the air, land and sea. The sun's heat causes water to **evaporate** – to rise from seas and lakes in the form of a gas – **water vapour**. The tiny water droplets gather to form clouds which drift over the land. As the warm, moist air rises over hills and mountains, it cools. The water vapour **condenses** and rain falls. Some rain is absorbed by plants. The rest trickles underground or is channelled into rivers. These rivers empty into the sea where the sun's heat causes the water to evaporate, so the cycle can begin again.

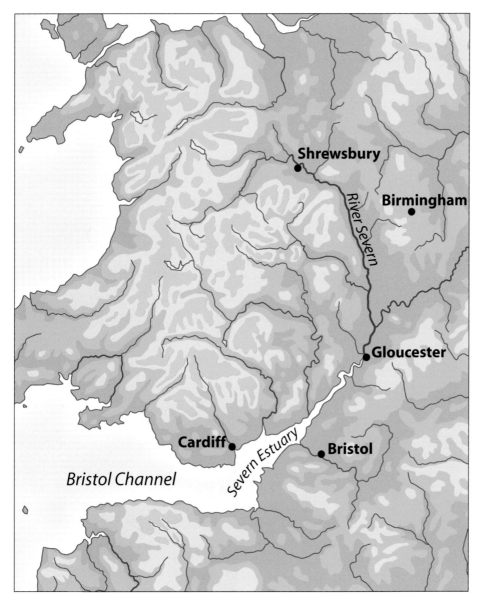

This map shows the **drainage basin** of the River Severn, Britain's longest river. It flows 354 km from the Welsh mountains to the Bristol Channel.

The mighty Amazon

The River Amazon has the world's largest drainage basin, covering 7,180,000 sq km – that's 40 per cent of South America! This vast river contains a fifth of all the water flowing in rivers anywhere in the world.

DETECTIVE WORK

Study the map of the River Severn or a map of your local river. Can you spot the following features: the source, a tributary, a confluence, the outlet, the drainage basin? To find out more about the River Severn, go to:

weblinks

www.waylinks.co.uk/series/GeogDetective/Rivers

Underground water seeps through tiny holes and cracks in rocks such as chalk and sandstone. When water reaches a layer of rock, through which it cannot pass, it runs sideways. On reaching the surface it will break through the ground as a spring.

Why do you think most rivers begin in hills or mountains?

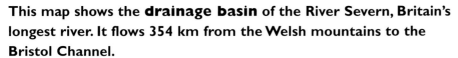

How do rivers shape the landscape?

Streams and rivers are the main force at work shaping the hills, mountains and valleys around us over thousands of years. High in the hills, rivers wear away the land they flow through, in a process called erosion. Downstream, rivers drop the sand and mud they are carrying to form new land near the mouth of the river.

In hills and mountains, the ground drops away steeply. Pulled by gravity, the water rushes downhill, loosening rocks and soil and carrying them away. Rocks and stones then act as the river's cutting tools, gouging deep, V-shaped valleys in the landscape. The materials carried along by the river are known as its **load**.

DETECTIVE WORK

Find out about how water erodes the soil by making a mini-mountain of heaped soil or sand, and trickling water over it. Watch how the water finds the quickest way downhill, wearing deep **gullies** in steep slopes.

Rocks and stones bouncing along the bed of rivers help to wear away deep gorges such as Kali Gandaki Gorge, in Nepal.

Waterfalls occur where rivers flow from hard rock to softer rock. The soft rock wears away more quickly, creating a sheer cliff over which the river drops. The force of tumbling water churns the rocks at the base, creating a deep pool.

Gradually, over thousands of years, the hard rock is undercut to form an overhang. Then the overhang collapses, and the waterfall moves a little further upstream.

At Niagara Falls in North America, the River Niagara plunges about 55 m in a huge, horseshoe-shaped falls.

Study the photo of Niagara. How do you think the waterfall might look in 1,000 years' time?

FOCUS ON

River deep, mountain high

Angel Falls in Venezuela, South America, is the world's highest waterfall, at 979 m high. The Kali Gandaki Gorge in Nepal is one of the world's deepest gorges, at 5.5 km deep.

Why don't rivers run straight?

As rivers leave the hills behind, the ground begins to slope more gently. As large boulders are dumped upstream by the river, it starts to flow more smoothly. Water naturally flows in a corkscrew motion, which makes the river weave like a snake.

Oxbow lakes don't usually last very long. **Sediment** gradually fills the lake to form a **swamp**.

More **tributaries** join the river and it becomes wider. The flowing water still has the energy to wear away the landscape, but it also starts to drop its **load** of sand and mud. This is called **deposition**. As the river curves through the landscape, the **current** flows fastest on the outside of bends, so these banks are cut away quickly. The flow is slower on the inside, so sand and mud are dropped here to form beaches and **shoals**.

A huge meander of the River Severn almost surrounds the city of Shrewsbury.

Study the photo of Shrewsbury. What are the advantages of the city's position? What might happen in times of flood?

As **erosion** and deposition continue, shallow curves become deep bends called **meanders**. Eventually only a narrow neck of land separates the wide loops. After heavy rain, the current becomes stronger. The river cuts right through the loop to form an **oxbow lake**. Over many years, more meanders form and slowly shift downstream.

Meander _____ _____ Oxbow lake

This picture shows how a meander develops. The powerful current on the outside of bends often wears the rock away to form steep sides of the river bank.

What happens as rivers approach the sea?

As rivers approach the sea, they mostly flow through a wide, flattish valley which has been worn by the winding river. This valley, called a flood plain, is covered by a thick layer of mud that has been dropped by the river when it floods. The deep, silty soil makes ideal farming land.

DETECTIVE WORK
Visit the mouth of your nearest river. Make drawings or take photos to record the scene at high and low tide. Can you find out the difference in water level between high and low tide? Try placing a marker, such as a coloured flag, at the point where the water is at its highest. Then measure how far the water has gone down in relation to the marker at low tide.

A spit, called Hurst Castle, lies at the mouth of the River Avon in southern England. This spit stretches out into the waters of the Solent.

The river is now carrying huge amounts of **sediment**: mostly soil washed from the banks, and small pieces of rock – the remains of boulders that have been smashed up by the river. As it reaches the deeper waters of the sea, the **current** slows. Sediment is deposited to form features such as **mudflats**, **spits** and **deltas** at the **mouth**.

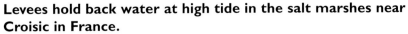

Levees hold back water at high tide in the salt marshes near Croisic in France.

The world's largest delta

The River Brahmaputra in Asia carries more sediment than any other river. The joint delta of the Ganges and Brahmaputra covers 75,000 sq km – that's over twice the size of Belgium. This area includes the Sundarbans – the world's largest swamp.

Spits are slender fingers of land stretching out to sea, shaped by ocean currents. Deltas are huge, fan-shaped areas of sediment dropped at the mouths of rivers such as the Mississippi – the river with the greatest quantity of water in North America. A river may split into several smaller channels, called **distributaries**, as it weaves through **swampland** to reach the sea.

Seawater floods the estuary of the River Lune in Lancashire at high tide. At low tide, the salt water drains away, leaving mudflats exposed on either side.

Study the photo of the spit in the Solent. Can you explain how the feature formed?

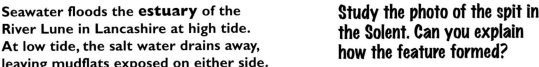

What kinds of wildlife inhabit rivers?

Rivers are home to many different kinds of plants, including floating weed and reeds, grasses and willows on the riverbank. Fish, tadpoles and young insects live in the water. Birds, frogs, mammals and even crocodiles may hunt along some river banks.

The bodies of aquatic (water-dwelling) animals are suited to living and moving in the water. Fish, beavers and crocodiles have flattened tails that push against the water. Ducks and otters have webbed feet that act as paddles. Many water creatures, such as fish, have a **streamlined** shape that aids swimming, while mammals, such as otters, have waterproof fur.

DETECTIVE WORK
Investigate the life in a river by gently sweeping a fishing net along the bottom. Put the creatures in a bucket of river water while you identify them using a wildlife book. Replace the animals gently when you've finished looking at them.

What features do birds have which make them suited to a watery habitat?

A hunting heron spreads its wings to lure fish into the shade.

The living things in the river depend on one another for food. Plants feed and grow using energy from sunlight. Plants and bits of dead matter provide food for small creatures such as shrimps, snails and worms, which may then be snapped up by fish. In turn, fish are eaten by larger hunters, such as herons, otters and people. The connections between river creatures can be shown in diagrams called **food chains**.

This diagram shows a simple river food chain.

Migrations

Some kinds of fish use rivers as highways as they travel on long journeys called **migrations**. Salmon grow-up in streams, swim out to sea as adults, and then return to their home stream to lay eggs. Eels move in the opposite direction, spending their lives in rivers, and then swimming out to sea to breed.

Salmon leap obstacles such as waterfalls as they move upriver to breed.

Why do people depend on rivers?

Plants, animals and people cannot survive without water. Artificial lakes, called **reservoirs**, are built to store river water for towns, and also for times when water is scarce. In **developed countries** like Britain, water flows from the tap whenever we turn it on. In some dry parts of the world like Africa, people have to walk for hours every day to fetch water. In developed countries, water is carefully cleaned before we use it. In poor countries, some people die from disease after drinking dirty water.

FOCUS ON

How much water?
In European countries, each person uses about 200 litres of water a day. That's 20 times the amount used by people in the world's poorest and driest countries. In the United States, people use even more – about 500 litres of water a day.

This African is drinking dirty water. Around 25 per cent of all the people in the world have to do without clean water.

People use water for cooking, cleaning and washing. **Sewage**, soap and detergents are flushed away. In developed countries, most waste water is filtered and cleaned before it is fed back into rivers. But sewage treatment is expensive, and some poorer countries cannot afford to clean their waste water properly before it flows back into rivers.

River water is also used by farmers to water crops and livestock. The world's main food crops – rice and wheat – need plenty of water to grow well. Thousands of years ago, farmers learned to channel river water onto fields to wet crops. This is called **irrigation**. Now 70 per cent of all the water taken from rivers is used in farming.

A farmer irrigates his crops in the Cotswolds, Britain.

DETECTIVE WORK

Work out how much water you use in a day. These measurements will help you:

Washing hands or cleaning teeth	5 litres
Flushing the toilet	10 litres
Five minute shower	75 litres
Dish washer	35 litres
Drinking water	2 litres
Bath	150 litres
Washing machine	250 litres

To learn more about how water is used in developing countries, go to:

weblinks

www.waylinks.co.uk/series/
GeogDetective/Rivers

How do we put rivers to work?

The water flowing in rivers has been used to drive machinery for centuries. Over 2,000 years ago, people began using water wheels to grind grain into flour. During the Industrial Revolution, in the eighteenth century, rivers were used in places like Britain to power looms to make cloth and factories sprang up on rivers all over Europe. Modern factories use river water for cleaning, cooling and other processes, and also to transport raw materials and finished goods.

Inside a hydroelectric power plant, rushing water is used to spin wheels called **turbines**, which power a generator, which then produces electricity.

River water is used in many industrial processes. However, factories on rivers can cause pollution (see pages 24-25).

The Three Gorges Dam on the Yangtze River will be one of the
world's biggest dams: 2 km long and 100 m high.

DETECTIVE WORK

Contact your local
electricity supplier to find
out what proportion of
their energy is generated
through hydroelectricity.
They may have a website
you could use. What
other methods are used
to generate electricity?

In the 1900s, people learned to
harness the power of rivers in a
new way. The energy of water
rushing down from hills and
mountains was harnessed to
generate electricity. This is called
hydroelectricity. A **dam** is
usually built above the
hydroelectric plant to control and
increase the force of the water.
Dams also help to prevent flooding,
but they alter river habitats.

FOCUS ON

Water in industry

Huge amounts of water
are used to make all
kinds of everyday
products, including paper,
cement and nylon. It
took over 15 litres of
water to make the paper
for this book; 180 litres
are needed to make a
sack of cement; 30,000
litres are needed to
make a car.

When a dam is built on a river, a huge **reservoir** builds up behind
it. In China, the huge Three Gorges Dam is being built on the
Yangtze River to generate electricity, and to prevent floods by
controlling the amount of water that flows downstream. The
finished dam will create a lake stretching 550 km upstream,
destroying wild habitats which are home to many different plants
and animals. Millions of people have had to abandon their homes
to make way for the dam.

How are rivers good for transportation?

Rivers have been used as transport routes for centuries. The first boats built by the Egyptians appeared on the River Nile over 5,000 years ago. Later, boats were also used by explorers to travel along rivers, particularly to penetrate densely forested areas like the Amazon Basin. Rivers provide a cheap way of transporting heavy and bulky goods such as minerals, crops and machinery. Huge amounts of freight now travel by river each year.

The first boats were simple rafts and canoes powered by sails or oars. In the 1800s, steam boats appeared on rivers like the Mississippi. Now all kinds of boats, from tugs, barges, yachts and speedboats to ocean-going liners, may be seen on rivers.

A cargo barge travels on the River Rhine.

FOCUS ON

The River Rhine

The River Rhine, flowing from Switzerland to the Netherlands, is one of Europe's busiest rivers. The river has been deepened so 800 km of the river's length can be used by ships. A canal has been built to link the Rhine with the River Danube to the east.

DETECTIVE WORK

To begin, find the River Rhine on a map of western Europe. Use a ruler on the map to measure the distance from the source of the Rhine to the mouth as if the river were to flow in a straight line. Now trace the river's wandering course with a piece of string, and measure it. How much do the twists and turns of the river add to its length? To find out more about the River Rhine, go to:

weblinks

www.waylinks.co.uk/series/
GeogDetective/Rivers

In their natural state, most rivers present hazards and dangers for shipping. Waterfalls, fast **currents**, **meanders**, **shoals** and rocks can all delay or damage boats. Many rivers have been altered to overcome these problems. Shallow rivers are **dredged** to make them deeper. Weirs and locks are used so that boats can pass by waterfalls.

In many countries, **canals** have been built to link rivers or straighten meanders. The 1700s to the 1800s was the great age of canal-building in Britain. Originally horses walked along the towpath to pull barges. Now diesel engines are mostly used instead.

Locks are built on canals to raise or lower the water level, so boats can pass up- or downstream.

Why are the paths next to canals in Britain called towpaths?

Why do towns develop near rivers?

Thousands of years ago, the first villages grew up along rivers in countries such as Iraq, Egypt and China. As well as water for drinking and farming, rivers yielded foods such as fish. Some held valuable minerals, such as gold or rock, that could be used for building. River plants, such as reeds and rushes, were used to make paper in Egyptian times and thatch houses in medieval times. Settlements on curved rivers were easy to defend.

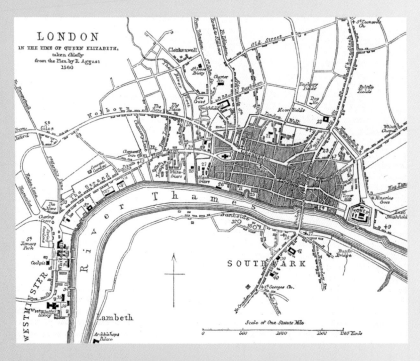

A substantial town surrounded the old walled town of Londinium, as this illustration from 1560 shows.

Compare the modern photograph of London with the old illustration. What changes have made it easier to cross the river?

The Roman settlement of Londinium now lies at the heart of a vast modern city.

DETECTIVE WORK

Draw a map from an aerial photo of London, showing key features along the river such as docks and bridges. Work out how the river affects transport by road and rail using the map. To find out more about the River Thames, go to:

weblinks

www.waylinks.co.uk/series/
GeogDetective/Rivers

As boats came to be used more and more, towns on rivers became busy ports, and later centres for manufacturing. Great trading centres, like London, grew up on the furthest point upstream that could be reached by ocean-going ships. Now many of the world's largest cities, including London, Paris, New York and Tokyo, are located on rivers or **estuaries**.

Rivers act as highways for ships, but they make transport across land more difficult. From early times, villages sprang up where rivers could be crossed safely, originally by wading across at **fords**. The names of British towns such as Oxford and Bedford show that they were once important crossing places. Bridges and, later, tunnels were also built to cross rivers. The first bridges were mostly wooden. Modern bridges are usually made of concrete, reinforced with steel.

Sea-going ships travel 1,600 km up the Amazon to dock at the port of Manaus.

FOCUS ON

The City of London

London, on the Thames, was founded by the Romans soon after they invaded Britain in 43 AD. The fortified town of Londinium was built at a crossing point that could be defended against enemies. By medieval times, London was a busy port and England's capital city.

Are people harming rivers?

Rivers are useful to people in hundreds of different ways: from providing a source of drinking water, to irrigating crops or transporting cargo. Unfortunately, human use of rivers often changes and sometimes harms aquatic habitats. The building of new towns, factories and power plants destroys stretches of river that were home to plants and animals. When mudflats, swamps and marshes are drained to make way for new farms or housing estates, water creatures have nowhere to live.

Pollution is a serious problem on many rivers. For centuries, towns, farms and factories have emptied **sewage** and other rubbish into rivers without thought for wildlife. Farmers use poisons called pesticides to kill crop-eating insects. When rain falls these pesticides trickle into rivers, killing water creatures. Dangerous waste from factories is sometimes dumped into rivers, where the poisons are absorbed by small creatures. When these are eaten by larger animals, the chemicals pass up the **food chain** (see pages 14-15).

DETECTIVE WORK

Run a health check on your local river. Dead fish, litter, scum, or green weed coating the surface are signs that the water may be polluted. However, freshwater shrimps and young insects called stoneflies only thrive in clear water. These minibeasts show that the river is not polluted. To find out more about how clean your local river is, go to:

weblinks

www.waylinks.co.uk/series/
GeogDetective/Rivers

Algae blanket the surface of the River Dene in Warwickshire, removing oxygen. Fish and other wildlife suffer as a result.

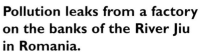

Pollution leaks from a factory on the banks of the River Jiu in Romania.

FOCUS ON

Mines

In the last decade, mines located on river banks have caused several serious accidents. In 1998, a spill of contaminated sludge from a mine killed wildlife along the Guadiamar River in Spain. In 2000, cyanide poison leaked from an old mine into two rivers in Romania. All water life died for 400 km downstream.

Fertilisers and sewage can make river water extra-rich in minerals that cause **algae** (tiny plants) to breed quickly. Green weed then smothers the surface, reducing the oxygen in the water, which can kill fish. Meanwhile, harmful gases released by cars, factories and power plants build up in the air to produce rain that is slightly acidic. When **acid rain** falls and drains into lakes and rivers, it can harm water life.

Litter spoils the beauty of rivers and can harm water life.

How can we take care of rivers?

Rivers are a precious resource, both for people and for wildlife. In many countries, governments, water companies and ordinary people are all taking steps to clean up rivers. Campaign groups such as Greenpeace tell people about pollution hazards. Water companies check water quality. Governments pass laws that prevent pollution and fine farms and factories that don't follow the rules.

DETECTIVE WORK

Ask your teacher if you can organise a class trip to clean up your local river. You'll need to wear gloves and wellingtons, and take care. Litter such as glass, tin cans and plastic bags can kill water creatures. Recycle the rubbish if you can.

In 2000, the south of England suffered severe flooding as rivers burst their banks following days of rain.

Everyone can help to reduce river pollution. Ask your family not to tip poisonous chemicals such as paint, oil and bleach down the drain, where they may pollute local water supplies. Your local authority can tell you how to get rid of these chemicals safely. As towns and cities grow, we all need to use water more carefully, and not waste it. You can save water by not leaving taps on, and by showering instead of having a bath.

Cleaning up the Thames

In Britain, tighter controls on pollution have improved the quality of the Thames around London. This river is now cleaner than it has been for centuries, and wildlife such as certain fish have returned.

Global warming is a new danger that is affecting rivers and other habitats. Waste gases from factories, cars and power stations are building up in the air to trap the sun's heat. This is making the **climate** warmer, and the weather unpredictable. Many dry places, such as countries in Africa, are receiving less rain, and rivers are drying up. Other areas, such as some parts of the USA, are receiving heavy rain, which makes rivers flood more often. Many countries are taking action to slow down global warming by reducing air pollution.

The gases that are causing global warming are known as greenhouse gases. Do you know why?

The Thames Barrier protects London against flooding. Global warming is making such defences vital.

Your project

If you've been doing detective work throughout the book, you should have gathered plenty of information about rivers. Bring it all together by producing your own project about rivers.

First you'll need to choose a topic that interests you. You could take one of the following questions as a starting point.

Many types of wildlife, such as this otter, live near rivers.

Topic questions

● How does your local river change as it flows from **source** to **outlet**? What features can be found along the river's course?

● How have people used rivers in the past, and how are rivers used today? *Or* compare use of a river in your area with river use in a different part of the world.

● The picture below shows an otter. What other kinds of wildlife can be found in rivers? How do plants or animals in European rivers differ from those in other parts of the world? How is human use of rivers affecting water life?

● The picture opposite shows a canoe. What other types of boats are found on rivers throughout the world? How are boat designs suited to conditions on the river?

Your local library and the Internet can provide all sorts of information to help you. Try the websites listed on page 31 for ideas. When you have gathered the information you need, present it in an interesting way. You might like to use one of the ideas below.

Project presentation

- Make a map of the river in the middle of a large piece of paper. Show the location of towns, bridges, factories, farms and docks along the river. Draw pictures around the edge, or place photographs showing scenes from the river's course.

- Write a report on the river from the point of view of one or more of the following people: a farmer, fisherman, town planner, factory-owner, **dam** architect, wildlife expert, prehistoric or medieval river-dweller.

- Imagine you are making a television documentary about the river. Plan a structure to explain all about it to viewers who know nothing about rivers.

A pair of canoeists glide down the upper Missouri River in Montana, USA.

Sherlock Bones has produced a project about river mammals, including otters, beavers, voles and river dolphins. He has found out that some river mammals are in trouble because of hunting or changes to their habitat.

Glossary

Acid rain Rain that is acidic because it is polluted by waste gases from factories, cars and power stations.

Algae Tiny plants that grow in water or damp places.

Canal An artificial waterway.

Climate The long-term weather conditions in a region.

Condense When water changes from a gas into a liquid.

Confluence The point where two rivers join.

Current A regular flow of water in a certain direction.

Dam A wall built across a river to hold back water.

Delta A fan-shaped area of land that forms as a river drops sediment at its mouth.

Deposition When a river drops its load of rocky fragments and sediment.

Developed countries The richer countries of the world, whose industries are well-developed.

Developing countries The poorer nations of the world, whose industries are less well developed.

Distributary One of the small channels into which a river divides as it nears the sea.

Drainage basin The total area drained by a river and its tributaries.

Dredge To deepen a river by removing mud and waste.

Erosion When rock or soil is worn away by the action of wind, rain or ice.

Estuary The mouth or lower stretch of a river, regularly washed by salty seawater.

Evaporate When water changes from a liquid into a gas.

Flood plain A flat plain bordering a river, covered with mud deposited by the river when it floods.

Food chain The name given to describe how plants and animals in an environment depend on each other for food.

Ford The shallow point where a river can be crossed by wading through it.

Glacier A river of ice found in mountain and polar regions.

Global warming A general rise in world temperatures, caused by a build-up of pollution in the atmosphere.

Gully A deep channel worn down by a river.

Hydroelectricity Electricity that is made using energy from fast-flowing water.

Irrigation When farmers water their fields in order to grow crops.

Levee A high bank edging a river, made of silt dropped by the river when it floods.

Load The rocky fragments carried along by a river, including boulders, pebbles, sand and mud.

Meander A looping bend in a river.

Migration A regular journey undertaken by an animal to avoid cold or find food or a safe place to breed.

Mouth (of a river) The place where a river meets the sea.

Mudflat A low-lying bank often found at the mouth of a river, and made of clay or silt.

Outlet The mouth of a river, where it flows into the sea or a lake.

Oxbow lake A crescent-shaped lake that forms when a deep loop in a river is cut off.

Reservoir An artificial lake used to store water or increase the power generated by a hydroelectric plant.

River system A unit made up of a river and all its streams and tributaries.

Sediment Fine rocky material, such as sand or mud.

Sewage Dirty water from homes, containing chemicals and human waste.

Shoal A group of fish that swim together.

Silt Fine pieces of rock that have been ground down to form clay, sand or mud.

Source The place where a river begins, such as a spring or lake.

Spit A long, slender finger of land stretching out into the sea or a river.

Streamlined Of animals with a slim, smooth body shape that slips easily through water.

Swamp A marshy area.

Tributary A small side river that joins the main river.

Turbine A machine powered by steam, gas or water that is used to generate electricity.

Water vapour Water in the form of a gas.

Answers

Page 4 Rivers are mainly fed by rain draining off the land into rivers or the streams that feed them. Some rivers dry up if no rain falls for months.

Page 7 Rivers mostly begin in hills and mountains because rainfall is heavy there. This is because as warm, moist air rises over high ground it cools, and the moisture **condenses** to fall as rain.

Page 9 Niagara Falls is moving upstream at a rate of more than a metre a year. So, in 1,000 years' time the falls may be sited about 1 km upstream.

Page 11 Water forms a natural barrier that made Shrewsbury

easy to defend. However, after heavy rain the river might one day cut right through the loop to flood the city.

Page 13 The spit of Hurst Castle is made of rocky debris worn from nearby cliffs or carried out to sea by the River Avon. Ocean currents have shifted the sediment to form the long spit.

Page 14 The heron's long legs allow it to wade through the water. Its long beak jabs forward to capture fish.

Page 21 These paths are called towpaths because they were originally used by horses towing barges.

Answer to detective work on page 21: The Rhine flows for 1,390 km. The distance from the **source** to the **mouth**, if the river were to flow in a straight line, is around 600 km. So, the river's winding course adds nearly 800 km to its length.

Page 22 London now has many more bridges, including road, foot and railway bridges. There are also several tunnels. The first tunnel under the Thames was opened in 1843.

page 27 Greenhouse gases are so-called because they act like glass in a greenhouse, trapping the sun's heat near the earth's surface. These gases include carbon dioxide and methane.

Further information

Books to read
Mandy Ross, *Geography Fact Files: Rivers* (Hodder Wayland, 2004)
Chris Oxlade, *Earth Files: Rivers and Lakes* (Heinemann, 2002)
Jen Green, *Saving Water* (Hodder Wayland, 2005)
Neil Morris, *Our World: Water* (Belitha, 2002)
Jane and Steve Parker, *Rivers* (Franklin Watts, 1997)

Websites:
International Rivers Network:
www.irn.org

World Conservation Monitoring Centre: www.wcmc.org.uk

Database on world's fresh water
www.worldwater.org/

Environmental Investigation Agency: www.eiainternational.org

Friends of the Earth
www.foe.co.uk

Greenpeace
www.greenpeace.org

Wateraid
www.wateraid.org.uk

Index